BUT

I

STILL

LOVE

YOU

TANUSH SINGHAL

Copyright © Tanush singhal 2025

Made with ❤ on the Notion Press Platform

www.notionpress.com

For my mother,

You raised a lover boy

Dear readers,

I hope this book gives you the feeling of being in love and the sadness it brings when you don't have the love you desire to be yours.

May you all find the love that once you thought didn't exist for you.

"Yaad aayegi har roz magar

Tujhe awaaz nah dunga,

Likhuga har shayari tere liye,

Par tera naam nah lunga"

- Jaun Elia

You are the stars of my night,

Moon to my sunshine

Waves to my river

Gaze at my eyes

Love to my sad side

The one to my zero

Flowers to my thorns

Happiness to my loneliness

Smile to my sad life

You are everything in my life.

It's the presence that made me feel alive

The presence reminded me that

I was a human with love

Who can love you.

The only presence I crave

And will always be craving for you

I miss you..

The person not willing to accept a new person in life

Now, he is willing to give his life for you

Just to give you the world's cutest smile

The smile that has taken my heart away

From me to you…

And that's when I knew.

The time I first saw you.

Glittering in that suit

Walking like an angel

With open hairs

That you are the one

That's when I knew

The time I saw you

Everything stopped around

With the feeling of nervousness

And the shyness popped up

The butterflies in my stomach

Giving the sensation

With the hint that you are the one.

I made you grow in my heart

But the roots strength our spell cast

You survived till the last

But I am not made for you at last

You will be the past

That going to shake my innocent heart.

And here I am

Healing her past scars

Making her mine

Day by day

Giving her the life

She deserved

Doing the things

she loved

Making her feels

How love works

Giving her time

In making me hers

Gonna sit down one evening.

Will tell you about

How I learn to love

What I got in love

How much my heart broke

How many hearts I made

How many pains I made mine

I love you no matter what happens to us

I know this is the end for you

But for me, this is the beginning

The beginning of a beautiful and peaceful journey

A beginning of being patient

A guy who hates waiting

Now going to wait for you

Just to have you in his life

Maybe this is not our time

Maybe in the future will be

Or maybe in another life

But for me, you are my only love...

No one says that love gives sadness, everyone says that it's a beautiful feeling to get but honestly love also brings sadness of not being together when you both need each other in the situation that you are suffering.

I know you have done everything to make me hate you but this heart doesn't want to hate you because you were the best feeling he has felt.

15

The flower you gave me is kept between the pages of my journal.

I pretend not to love you anymore, but catch myself opening those pages every once in a while.

Reading the paras I wrote for you,

Letting me think that one day you will return,

To read what I wrote for you.

Not loving you is not an option for me

Because when I try to,

I find myself opening those folders

I hid in my phone

Admiring the beauty of yours,

As I am not able to see you anymore.

I don't love you anymore is just a lie

Because I love you every day more and more...

Never letting that love slip away from me,

It's the only thing I kept after you left.

It was when you became special to me

Its when I gave you the place that no one has taken from me

It is when you become as important as nobody else

It was when you made me happy

It was when you called me yours

It was when I called you mine

It's us that will be forever of each other

It's us that no misunderstanding can separate us

It is that we fight but solve it as we can't live without each other

It's me who always gets mad but,

It's you who always handled me

It's us who always made sweet memories together...

It's the day when I first saw you

It's the day when I fall for your eyes

It's me who approached you

It's you who ignored me

It's your smile that gives me a chill every time

It's me who always takes the first step in a
conversation

It's you who always gives me dry replies

It's me who fell for you harder

It's me who made you fall for me even harder

It's us that we are now together…

Just like trees shed their leaves to give space for the new ones to bloom

Same for us we have to forget our past to give space to the new ones...

And there I lost

My consciousness

Lost in her eyes

Staring at my future wife

Glamouring in sunlight

Those coffee-brown eyes

Made me smile every time

Staring at me with them

Makes my heart beat quiet

I love those coffee-brown eyes...

There, I lost my consciousness.

Gazing at my phone

First time seeing in her in a saree,

So divine,

Glittering like blue ocean shine

With sunlight glowing on her face

Making my expressions fade,

Forcing myself not to stare,

But couldn't resist

She shone like an angel from heaven's mist

Princess of my heart's kingdom, queen of my dreams,

I lost my life to her, it seems

Now everything belongs to her

My soul finds in her..

And here I am

Staring at her pic

Thinking what good things

I have done

That I got her

Don't know what

but yeah I know

She is the one

That I wanna keep forever

Yeah I know forever is nothing

Still want her till my last breath

Want her till my last 7 mins

The mins mind play before we die...

If I could turn back time,

I would go back to when you wanted to be mine

The time we shared when love was new,

When we spent moments together,

Just me and you.

The time your care wrapped me tight,

The time your presence made

Everything right.

The time your smile lit up my day,

The time you were my home,

Every step of the way

The time I was your boy, full of cheers,

The time I was happy, with you always near...

Waiting,

What a word…

Most of the people hate waiting but when they fell in love the learn to wait for the person they love.

Love

That simple four-letter word comes with lots of patience and calmness. This simple word teaches the person to be patient and calm at the moments when he was unable to be calmed.

Hope

A word that changes the way you think in love. This word plays a crucial role when the person leaves you but still holds on to that 0.01% hope that the person will return. This hope will become your way of living for that person.

You are the sunshine to my dark

The flower to my empty vase

The home I will crave till last...

I am a firm believer in destiny,

So, if destiny decides our paths will cross again….

Though we're no longer talking anymore,
Because you were gone very far from me,
A part of me remains yours, every single day.
We've returned each other's belongings but your essence stays,
Reminding of you each evening, in every way.
There's a folder on my phone, filled with memories of you,
A place I visit every night, to see the smile I once knew.
To the smile, I have given myself up.

Perhaps I'm just a fleeting presence in your life,
But for me, you are my last love, my last strife.
Whom I had given my heart,
You were the one I loved the most.
You were the home I gave up on everything,
But you are the one that took the life out of me
leaving nothing.
Still, you're my last love.
For whom I'll yearn, till you utterly consume me
and I'm but a name.

And there I stood
Frozen in time
Seeing the person leave
While pieces of heart in my hand
Until they got flushed
By the rain of my tears
Remembering the weight
They hold with every drop.
Making my soul torn apart
Leaving me with the Hollow
Aching heart
The anguish is palpable.
The grief was almost suffocating.
And seeing myself crumbling away
Just like sand slipping from hand
With every grain of sand
A memory fades
Leaving only sorrowful shades

Though I can't see you anymore
But the moon reminds me of your eyes.
Which made me forget the challenges and strife
Yeah, I am unable to forget you.
For an internal part of me still belongs to you.
But I still love you...

I was a man with a lot of sins but you came into my life like an angel who rectified my sins.

Today, when I was sick, I remember the day when you were there for me and taking care of me just like my mom. But today is something different as you know about but you didn't even care about it.

When I am on my deathbed

Don't come close to me.

I am not able to wipe your tears

And make you smile again...

I know when I am dead...

I will be breaking all my promises i.e.

Be with you forever

Don't leave your side

I am telling you

After me, you take my phone with you...

Whenever you miss me

Just read old chats of us and listen to

fav music of us...

It will make you feel that I am there always...

And don't cry whenever you miss me

I will not be able to make you happy again...

Make you smile again...

So don't lose your smile for me...

Always be smiling...

Stages of love:

There are different stages in love

Let's say you met someone You started talking the first day if you have a good conversation skill you can make it a good conversation but if not, that can be a very awkward conversation for you.

If that people make you feel butterflies when you are talking to them that means you start developing feelings for them. That moment is different for everyone and that phase is something else.

You talking to them and giggling while talking. Those blushing on your cheeks it's different. Then comes the confession phase

In this phase, you confess your feelings, and if both of them have the same feelings it goes forward. This phase may be rough for most of them as sometimes people misunderstand the feelings of the other person.

People say love only happens once but it can happen twice in your lifetime don't consider attraction as love there is a lot of difference between these two terms.

Love is something that comes slowly to you and when it comes you will not understand there is always another person who makes you realize that you are in love. You started doing silly things in love. You make sacrifices and compromises for that person and make them feel special every time whenever they are around you.

I still remember our first date; you were blossoming like blue orchids (my fav flowers) in the blue top with a butterfly sticker on it complimenting the look of yours as you always give me those butterflies whenever you are around me. You are that butterfly in my life that gave me the hope to live life happily.

I am the writer,

You are the muse that sparks my pen.

But one fateful day, I lost my muse,

And in that silence, my words grew dim.

Once vibrant verses flowed like streams,

Now they linger in shadows, void of dreams.

For without your light, my inspiration wanes,

And the heart of my writing grows weary with chains.

I still have the letters I wrote for you. I write a letter every day describing my day for you as it was our schedule when we were together. When you left the spark of my day was gone because you were the only thing that kept me going.

Sometimes, letting them go is the only option left because you can't forcefully keep the person in your life.

Sometimes, letting them go is the only option left because you can't forcefully keep the person in your life.

Loving someone from far away has a unique way of expressing it. Only one side lover can understand this.

Love teaches you so many lessons but one of the lessons of love is sacrificing. This lesson comes with a lot of pain and suffering as you have to sacrifice many things to maintain and move forward with love.

I still have the shirt that I gave you, haven't washed it because it contains the essence of you which reminds me that I still have the hope to have you in my life.

You delight in teasing me before my kin,

Causing my cheeks to bloom, a sweet, rosy sin.

Now, their laughter dances upon your name,

But I can't reveal it's no longer the same.

The day I forget you,

It is the day I die for you.

You were the melody of my day

Without you, the silence felt grey

For your wish, I tried to forget,

But found myself re-reading the words you'd set.

The paragraphs you wrote, just for me,

Especially the line, 'You mean a lot to me'

When you called at midnight, my phone lay still,

Silent and dark, with no whisper to fulfill.

But when I woke, the missed call shone bright,

Fear gripped my heart; it was a terrifying sight.

The thought of losing you caught me off guard,

A hundred thoughts collided.

My heart raced wildly as if it would leap out instead,

A loss I fear that my heart just can't bear.

For your sake, I tried to give a chance to another,

But it's hard to open up to someone I don't love.

The love of my life remains with you,

The one who's far away from me.

My last wish was to fulfill yours,

To give a chance to someone new.

But, my love, my heart still belongs to you.

Those eyes,

Those glittering coffee-brown eyes,

The day I saw them

Made me fall for them,

Consuming my world within their depths.

Those eyes possess a power over me;

Whenever I see them, I forget everything.

The innocence they hold

Is a child they are afraid to reveal.

Killing myself a little to write a bit about you cuz remembering the time together makes me feel empty without you…

Yeah, I deleted all your pics from my phone,

But one piece of you remains, forever my own.

A single photo in my wallet, I hold tight,

A constant reminder, day and night.

I don't have the power to let it go,

'Cause you're the one I'll always hold on to, no
matter what I know.'

Writing about love becomes a fierce struggle when the one you cherish is absent from your life.

The day I put your picture in my wallet, I was so excited to tell you about it. Now, even though everything else has changed, your picture remains in its place because I don't want to remove anything — it's a reminder of what's gone. One thing is true: I love you, and I will continue to love you whether you are with me or not.

In shadows cast where dreams take flight,

A girl once sparked my soul's delight.

With visions bright and hopes so grand,

She held my heart, took my hand.

Ambitions soared on whispered air,

A tapestry of love and care.

Yet now as triumph's dawn draws near,

Her absence whispers, sharp and clear.

In every step, her spirit sways,

In bittersweet, my heart obeys.

For though the prize may soon be mine,

Without her light, it can't truly shine.

If you loved the book, Please leave a note in my DM

@the_tanushdiaries

Acknowledgment

For you CUPCAKE,
I have written this book for you. I know we are not talking anymore,

"But I still love you"

Mehak, my best friend, there are many things for which I could thank you, but the only thing I will thank you for is handling me and listening to my tantrum at 3 a.m. You are the best.

Avni, my sister, whom I call whenever I am in trouble. I can't thank you enough for always being there for me and constantly supporting me in every situation.

A special thanks to my friend and enemy, Mansi, for always being there on the call when I am stuck or feeling anxious. Always giving me input in the book and being the first one to read it. Thank you so much for the late-night calls and the funny banter. I hate you :)

Rohan, my mentor, I am truly enjoying my time in the corporate world with you. Your cool and awesome demeanor makes a significant impact. Thank you for your unwavering support.